This book belongs to the one and only

____

If found please contact here

____

____

____

Published by Crackerjack Books

This notebook is perfect for keeping your internet passwords, login and other information safe and secure.

All the way back to the ancient Greeks the white rose has been a symbol of privacy, secrecy and confidentiality. The Latin expression "sub rosa" means "under the seal of secrecy", literally meaning "under the rose". This wonderful little **"White Rose Secrets"** notebook keeps to that tradition and could really be a lifesaver!

Are you woefully awful at remembering logins and passwords? How many times have you changed, lost or forgotten a website password or login? Or changed your PC without backing up. Or had your portable storage backup device corrupted without another backup of your backup, poof, gone! Also, many companies are moving exclusively to online statements and payments so it can be really tough to keep track of them all, and maybe you don't want to "save" your login information on your laptop or PC for security reasons.

For extra security and peace of mind you should keep all your important, valuable passwords organized, safe and secure in this useful logbook journal and then keep it in a safe and secure place. Plus if anything were to happen to you, your family can access your social media and financial accounts to make any necessary arrangements.

There is ample space for listing all your internet sites and accounts, usernames, password hints, PINs, security questions and additional notes like ISP settings and serial numbers.

The **"White Rose Secrets"** password logbook with a non-descriptive cover is the perfect organizational means to make your life easier and a nice gift to give to others.

Disclaimer: Please be aware that any information you write down in this book is very important and therefore you will need to protect carefully so it doesn't fall into the wrong hands.

It is your responsibility to keep it safe and secure.

By using this book you acknowledge and agree that you are accountable for any and all information stored in it. Accordingly, you agree that the author and publisher are not liable in any way for any damages resulting from unauthorized use, loss or theft of the book or any wrongful use of the information in your book.

SITE	A

URL:

USERNAME:

PASSWORD:

EMAIL:

CATEGORY:

NOTE:

SITE

URL:

USERNAME:

PASSWORD:

EMAIL:

CATEGORY:

NOTE:

SITE

URL:

USERNAME:

PASSWORD:

EMAIL:

CATEGORY:

NOTE:

SITE

URL:

USERNAME:

PASSWORD:

EMAIL:

CATEGORY:

NOTE:

SITE

URL:

USERNAME:

PASSWORD:

EMAIL:

CATEGORY:

NOTE:

SITE

URL:

USERNAME:

PASSWORD:

EMAIL:

CATEGORY:

NOTE:

SITE

URL:

USERNAME:

PASSWORD:

EMAIL:

CATEGORY:

NOTE:

SITE

URL:

USERNAME:

PASSWORD:

EMAIL:

CATEGORY:

NOTE:

SITE

URL:

USERNAME:

PASSWORD:

EMAIL:

CATEGORY:

NOTE:

SITE

URL:

USERNAME:

PASSWORD:

EMAIL:

CATEGORY:

NOTE:

SITE

URL:

USERNAME:

PASSWORD:

EMAIL:

CATEGORY:

NOTE:

SITE

URL:

USERNAME:

PASSWORD:

EMAIL:

CATEGORY:

NOTE:

SITE

URL:

USERNAME:

PASSWORD:

EMAIL:

CATEGORY:

NOTE:

SITE

URL:

USERNAME:

PASSWORD:

EMAIL:

CATEGORY:

NOTE:

SITE

URL:

USERNAME:

PASSWORD:

EMAIL:

CATEGORY:

NOTE:

SITE

URL:

USERNAME:

PASSWORD:

EMAIL:

CATEGORY:

NOTE:

SITE

URL:

USERNAME:

PASSWORD:

EMAIL:

CATEGORY:

NOTE:

SITE

URL:

USERNAME:

PASSWORD:

EMAIL:

CATEGORY:

NOTE:

SITE

URL:

USERNAME:

PASSWORD:

EMAIL:

CATEGORY:

NOTE:

SITE

URL:

USERNAME:

PASSWORD:

EMAIL:

CATEGORY:

NOTE:

SITE

URL:

USERNAME:

PASSWORD:

EMAIL:

CATEGORY:

NOTE:

SITE

URL:

USERNAME:

PASSWORD:

EMAIL:

CATEGORY:

NOTE:

SITE

URL:

USERNAME:

PASSWORD:

EMAIL:

CATEGORY:

NOTE:

SITE

URL:

USERNAME:

PASSWORD:

EMAIL:

CATEGORY:

NOTE:

SITE

URL:

USERNAME:

PASSWORD:

EMAIL:

CATEGORY:

NOTE:

SITE

URL:

USERNAME:

PASSWORD:

EMAIL:

CATEGORY:

NOTE:

SITE

URL:

USERNAME:

PASSWORD:

EMAIL:

CATEGORY:

NOTE:

SITE

URL:

USERNAME:

PASSWORD:

EMAIL:

CATEGORY:

NOTE:

SITE

URL:

USERNAME:

PASSWORD:

EMAIL:

CATEGORY:

NOTE:

SITE

URL:

USERNAME:

PASSWORD:

EMAIL:

CATEGORY:

NOTE:

SITE

URL:

USERNAME:

PASSWORD:

EMAIL:

CATEGORY:

NOTE:

SITE

URL:

USERNAME:

PASSWORD:

EMAIL:

CATEGORY:

NOTE:

<table>
<tr><td colspan="2">SITE</td></tr>
<tr><td>URL:</td></tr>
<tr><td>USERNAME:</td></tr>
<tr><td>PASSWORD:</td></tr>
<tr><td>EMAIL:</td></tr>
<tr><td>CATEGORY:</td></tr>
<tr><td>NOTE:</td></tr>
</table>

<table>
<tr><td colspan="2">SITE</td></tr>
<tr><td>URL:</td></tr>
<tr><td>USERNAME:</td></tr>
<tr><td>PASSWORD:</td></tr>
<tr><td>EMAIL:</td></tr>
<tr><td>CATEGORY:</td></tr>
<tr><td>NOTE:</td></tr>
</table>

<table>
<tr><td colspan="2">SITE</td></tr>
<tr><td>URL:</td></tr>
<tr><td>USERNAME:</td></tr>
<tr><td>PASSWORD:</td></tr>
<tr><td>EMAIL:</td></tr>
<tr><td>CATEGORY:</td></tr>
<tr><td>NOTE:</td></tr>
</table>

<table>
<tr><td colspan="2">SITE</td></tr>
<tr><td>URL:</td></tr>
<tr><td>USERNAME:</td></tr>
<tr><td>PASSWORD:</td></tr>
<tr><td>EMAIL:</td></tr>
<tr><td>CATEGORY:</td></tr>
<tr><td>NOTE:</td></tr>
</table>

SITE

URL:

USERNAME:

PASSWORD:

EMAIL:

CATEGORY:

NOTE:

SITE

URL:

USERNAME:

PASSWORD:

EMAIL:

CATEGORY:

NOTE:

SITE

URL:

USERNAME:

PASSWORD:

EMAIL:

CATEGORY:

NOTE:

SITE

URL:

USERNAME:

PASSWORD:

EMAIL:

CATEGORY:

NOTE:

SITE

URL:

USERNAME:

PASSWORD:

EMAIL:

CATEGORY:

NOTE:

SITE

URL:

USERNAME:

PASSWORD:

EMAIL:

CATEGORY:

NOTE:

SITE

URL:

USERNAME:

PASSWORD:

EMAIL:

CATEGORY:

NOTE:

SITE

URL:

USERNAME:

PASSWORD:

EMAIL:

CATEGORY:

NOTE:

SITE

URL:

USERNAME:

PASSWORD:

EMAIL:

CATEGORY:

NOTE:

SITE

URL:

USERNAME:

PASSWORD:

EMAIL:

CATEGORY:

NOTE:

SITE

URL:

USERNAME:

PASSWORD:

EMAIL:

CATEGORY:

NOTE:

SITE

URL:

USERNAME:

PASSWORD:

EMAIL:

CATEGORY:

NOTE:

SITE

URL:

USERNAME:

PASSWORD:

EMAIL:

CATEGORY:

NOTE:

SITE

URL:

USERNAME:

PASSWORD:

EMAIL:

CATEGORY:

NOTE:

SITE

URL:

USERNAME:

PASSWORD:

EMAIL:

CATEGORY:

NOTE:

SITE

URL:

USERNAME:

PASSWORD:

EMAIL:

CATEGORY:

NOTE:

SITE
URL:
USERNAME:
PASSWORD:
EMAIL:
CATEGORY:
NOTE:

SITE
URL:
USERNAME:
PASSWORD:
EMAIL:
CATEGORY:
NOTE:

SITE
URL:
USERNAME:
PASSWORD:
EMAIL:
CATEGORY:
NOTE:

SITE
URL:
USERNAME:
PASSWORD:
EMAIL:
CATEGORY:
NOTE:

SITE	
URL:	
USERNAME:	
PASSWORD:	
EMAIL:	
CATEGORY:	
NOTE:	

SITE	
URL:	
USERNAME:	
PASSWORD:	
EMAIL:	
CATEGORY:	
NOTE:	

SITE	
URL:	
USERNAME:	
PASSWORD:	
EMAIL:	
CATEGORY:	
NOTE:	

SITE	
URL:	
USERNAME:	
PASSWORD:	
EMAIL:	
CATEGORY:	
NOTE:	

SITE

URL:

USERNAME:

PASSWORD:

EMAIL:

CATEGORY:

NOTE:

SITE

URL:

USERNAME:

PASSWORD:

EMAIL:

CATEGORY:

NOTE:

SITE

URL:

USERNAME:

PASSWORD:

EMAIL:

CATEGORY:

NOTE:

SITE

URL:

USERNAME:

PASSWORD:

EMAIL:

CATEGORY:

NOTE:

SITE

URL:

USERNAME:

PASSWORD:

EMAIL:

CATEGORY:

NOTE:

SITE

URL:

USERNAME:

PASSWORD:

EMAIL:

CATEGORY:

NOTE:

SITE

URL:

USERNAME:

PASSWORD:

EMAIL:

CATEGORY:

NOTE:

SITE

URL:

USERNAME:

PASSWORD:

EMAIL:

CATEGORY:

NOTE:

SITE

URL:

USERNAME:

PASSWORD:

EMAIL:

CATEGORY:

NOTE:

SITE

URL:

USERNAME:

PASSWORD:

EMAIL:

CATEGORY:

NOTE:

SITE

URL:

USERNAME:

PASSWORD:

EMAIL:

CATEGORY:

NOTE:

SITE

URL:

USERNAME:

PASSWORD:

EMAIL:

CATEGORY:

NOTE:

SITE

URL:

USERNAME:

PASSWORD:

EMAIL:

CATEGORY:

NOTE:

SITE

URL:

USERNAME:

PASSWORD:

EMAIL:

CATEGORY:

NOTE:

SITE

URL:

USERNAME:

PASSWORD:

EMAIL:

CATEGORY:

NOTE:

SITE

URL:

USERNAME:

PASSWORD:

EMAIL:

CATEGORY:

NOTE:

SITE

URL:

USERNAME:

PASSWORD:

EMAIL:

CATEGORY:

NOTE:

SITE

URL:

USERNAME:

PASSWORD:

EMAIL:

CATEGORY:

NOTE:

SITE

URL:

USERNAME:

PASSWORD:

EMAIL:

CATEGORY:

NOTE:

SITE

URL:

USERNAME:

PASSWORD:

EMAIL:

CATEGORY:

NOTE:

SITE

URL:

USERNAME:

PASSWORD:

EMAIL:

CATEGORY:

NOTE:

SITE

URL:

USERNAME:

PASSWORD:

EMAIL:

CATEGORY:

NOTE:

SITE

URL:

USERNAME:

PASSWORD:

EMAIL:

CATEGORY:

NOTE:

SITE

URL:

USERNAME:

PASSWORD:

EMAIL:

CATEGORY:

NOTE:

SITE

URL:

USERNAME:

PASSWORD:

EMAIL:

CATEGORY:

NOTE:

SITE

URL:

USERNAME:

PASSWORD:

EMAIL:

CATEGORY:

NOTE:

SITE

URL:

USERNAME:

PASSWORD:

EMAIL:

CATEGORY:

NOTE:

SITE

URL:

USERNAME:

PASSWORD:

EMAIL:

CATEGORY:

NOTE:

SITE

URL:

USERNAME:

PASSWORD:

EMAIL:

CATEGORY:

NOTE:

SITE

URL:

USERNAME:

PASSWORD:

EMAIL:

CATEGORY:

NOTE:

SITE

URL:

USERNAME:

PASSWORD:

EMAIL:

CATEGORY:

NOTE:

SITE

URL:

USERNAME:

PASSWORD:

EMAIL:

CATEGORY:

NOTE:

SITE
URL:
USERNAME:
PASSWORD:
EMAIL:
CATEGORY:
NOTE:

SITE
URL:
USERNAME:
PASSWORD:
EMAIL:
CATEGORY:
NOTE:

SITE
URL:
USERNAME:
PASSWORD:
EMAIL:
CATEGORY:
NOTE:

SITE
URL:
USERNAME:
PASSWORD:
EMAIL:
CATEGORY:
NOTE:

SITE

URL:

USERNAME:

PASSWORD:

EMAIL:

CATEGORY:

NOTE:

SITE

URL:

USERNAME:

PASSWORD:

EMAIL:

CATEGORY:

NOTE:

SITE

URL:

USERNAME:

PASSWORD:

EMAIL:

CATEGORY:

NOTE:

SITE

URL:

USERNAME:

PASSWORD:

EMAIL:

CATEGORY:

NOTE:

SITE

URL:

USERNAME:

PASSWORD:

EMAIL:

CATEGORY:

NOTE:

SITE

URL:

USERNAME:

PASSWORD:

EMAIL:

CATEGORY:

NOTE:

SITE

URL:

USERNAME:

PASSWORD:

EMAIL:

CATEGORY:

NOTE:

SITE

URL:

USERNAME:

PASSWORD:

EMAIL:

CATEGORY:

NOTE:

SITE

URL:

USERNAME:

PASSWORD:

EMAIL:

CATEGORY:

NOTE:

SITE

URL:

USERNAME:

PASSWORD:

EMAIL:

CATEGORY:

NOTE:

SITE

URL:

USERNAME:

PASSWORD:

EMAIL:

CATEGORY:

NOTE:

SITE

URL:

USERNAME:

PASSWORD:

EMAIL:

CATEGORY:

NOTE:

SITE

URL:

USERNAME:

PASSWORD:

EMAIL:

CATEGORY:

NOTE:

SITE

URL:

USERNAME:

PASSWORD:

EMAIL:

CATEGORY:

NOTE:

SITE

URL:

USERNAME:

PASSWORD:

EMAIL:

CATEGORY:

NOTE:

SITE

URL:

USERNAME:

PASSWORD:

EMAIL:

CATEGORY:

NOTE:

SITE

URL:

USERNAME:

PASSWORD:

EMAIL:

CATEGORY:

NOTE:

SITE

URL:

USERNAME:

PASSWORD:

EMAIL:

CATEGORY:

NOTE:

SITE

URL:

USERNAME:

PASSWORD:

EMAIL:

CATEGORY:

NOTE:

SITE

URL:

USERNAME:

PASSWORD:

EMAIL:

CATEGORY:

NOTE:

SITE

URL:

USERNAME:

PASSWORD:

EMAIL:

CATEGORY:

NOTE:

SITE

URL:

USERNAME:

PASSWORD:

EMAIL:

CATEGORY:

NOTE:

SITE

URL:

USERNAME:

PASSWORD:

EMAIL:

CATEGORY:

NOTE:

SITE

URL:

USERNAME:

PASSWORD:

EMAIL:

CATEGORY:

NOTE:

SITE

URL:

USERNAME:

PASSWORD:

EMAIL:

CATEGORY:

NOTE:

SITE

URL:

USERNAME:

PASSWORD:

EMAIL:

CATEGORY:

NOTE:

SITE

URL:

USERNAME:

PASSWORD:

EMAIL:

CATEGORY:

NOTE:

SITE

URL:

USERNAME:

PASSWORD:

EMAIL:

CATEGORY:

NOTE:

SITE	
URL:	
USERNAME:	
PASSWORD:	
EMAIL:	
CATEGORY:	
NOTE:	

SITE	
URL:	
USERNAME:	
PASSWORD:	
EMAIL:	
CATEGORY:	
NOTE:	

SITE	
URL:	
USERNAME:	
PASSWORD:	
EMAIL:	
CATEGORY:	
NOTE:	

SITE	
URL:	
USERNAME:	
PASSWORD:	
EMAIL:	
CATEGORY:	
NOTE:	

SITE
URL:
USERNAME:
PASSWORD:
EMAIL:
CATEGORY:
NOTE:

SITE
URL:
USERNAME:
PASSWORD:
EMAIL:
CATEGORY:
NOTE:

SITE
URL:
USERNAME:
PASSWORD:
EMAIL:
CATEGORY:
NOTE:

SITE
URL:
USERNAME:
PASSWORD:
EMAIL:
CATEGORY:
NOTE:

SITE

URL:

USERNAME:

PASSWORD:

EMAIL:

CATEGORY:

NOTE:

SITE

URL:

USERNAME:

PASSWORD:

EMAIL:

CATEGORY:

NOTE:

SITE

URL:

USERNAME:

PASSWORD:

EMAIL:

CATEGORY:

NOTE:

SITE

URL:

USERNAME:

PASSWORD:

EMAIL:

CATEGORY:

NOTE:

SITE	

URL:

USERNAME:

PASSWORD:

EMAIL:

CATEGORY:

NOTE:

SITE

URL:

USERNAME:

PASSWORD:

EMAIL:

CATEGORY:

NOTE:

SITE

URL:

USERNAME:

PASSWORD:

EMAIL:

CATEGORY:

NOTE:

SITE

URL:

USERNAME:

PASSWORD:

EMAIL:

CATEGORY:

NOTE:

SITE

URL:

USERNAME:

PASSWORD:

EMAIL:

CATEGORY:

NOTE:

SITE

URL:

USERNAME:

PASSWORD:

EMAIL:

CATEGORY:

NOTE:

SITE

URL:

USERNAME:

PASSWORD:

EMAIL:

CATEGORY:

NOTE:

SITE

URL:

USERNAME:

PASSWORD:

EMAIL:

CATEGORY:

NOTE:

SITE

URL:

USERNAME:

PASSWORD:

EMAIL:

CATEGORY:

NOTE:

SITE

URL:

USERNAME:

PASSWORD:

EMAIL:

CATEGORY:

NOTE:

SITE

URL:

USERNAME:

PASSWORD:

EMAIL:

CATEGORY:

NOTE:

SITE

URL:

USERNAME:

PASSWORD:

EMAIL:

CATEGORY:

NOTE:

SITE

URL:

USERNAME:

PASSWORD:

EMAIL:

CATEGORY:

NOTE:

SITE

URL:

USERNAME:

PASSWORD:

EMAIL:

CATEGORY:

NOTE:

SITE

URL:

USERNAME:

PASSWORD:

EMAIL:

CATEGORY:

NOTE:

SITE

URL:

USERNAME:

PASSWORD:

EMAIL:

CATEGORY:

NOTE:

SITE	
URL:	
USERNAME:	
PASSWORD:	
EMAIL:	
CATEGORY:	
NOTE:	

SITE	
URL:	
USERNAME:	
PASSWORD:	
EMAIL:	
CATEGORY:	
NOTE:	

SITE	
URL:	
USERNAME:	
PASSWORD:	
EMAIL:	
CATEGORY:	
NOTE:	

SITE	
URL:	
USERNAME:	
PASSWORD:	
EMAIL:	
CATEGORY:	
NOTE:	

SITE

URL:

USERNAME:

PASSWORD:

EMAIL:

CATEGORY:

NOTE:

SITE

URL:

USERNAME:

PASSWORD:

EMAIL:

CATEGORY:

NOTE:

SITE

URL:

USERNAME:

PASSWORD:

EMAIL:

CATEGORY:

NOTE:

SITE

URL:

USERNAME:

PASSWORD:

EMAIL:

CATEGORY:

NOTE:

SITE	

URL:

USERNAME:

PASSWORD:

EMAIL:

CATEGORY:

NOTE:

SITE	

URL:

USERNAME:

PASSWORD:

EMAIL:

CATEGORY:

NOTE:

SITE	

URL:

USERNAME:

PASSWORD:

EMAIL:

CATEGORY:

NOTE:

SITE	

URL:

USERNAME:

PASSWORD:

EMAIL:

CATEGORY:

NOTE:

SITE

URL:

USERNAME:

PASSWORD:

EMAIL:

CATEGORY:

NOTE:

SITE

URL:

USERNAME:

PASSWORD:

EMAIL:

CATEGORY:

NOTE:

SITE

URL:

USERNAME:

PASSWORD:

EMAIL:

CATEGORY:

NOTE:

SITE

URL:

USERNAME:

PASSWORD:

EMAIL:

CATEGORY:

NOTE:

SITE	
URL:	
USERNAME:	
PASSWORD:	
EMAIL:	
CATEGORY:	
NOTE:	

SITE	
URL:	
USERNAME:	
PASSWORD:	
EMAIL:	
CATEGORY:	
NOTE:	

SITE	
URL:	
USERNAME:	
PASSWORD:	
EMAIL:	
CATEGORY:	
NOTE:	

SITE	
URL:	
USERNAME:	
PASSWORD:	
EMAIL:	
CATEGORY:	
NOTE:	

SITE

URL:

USERNAME:

PASSWORD:

EMAIL:

CATEGORY:

NOTE:

SITE

URL:

USERNAME:

PASSWORD:

EMAIL:

CATEGORY:

NOTE:

SITE

URL:

USERNAME:

PASSWORD:

EMAIL:

CATEGORY:

NOTE:

SITE

URL:

USERNAME:

PASSWORD:

EMAIL:

CATEGORY:

NOTE:

SITE

URL:

USERNAME:

PASSWORD:

EMAIL:

CATEGORY:

NOTE:

SITE

URL:

USERNAME:

PASSWORD:

EMAIL:

CATEGORY:

NOTE:

SITE

URL:

USERNAME:

PASSWORD:

EMAIL:

CATEGORY:

NOTE:

SITE

URL:

USERNAME:

PASSWORD:

EMAIL:

CATEGORY:

NOTE:

	SITE
URL:	
USERNAME:	
PASSWORD:	
EMAIL:	
CATEGORY:	
NOTE:	

	SITE
URL:	
USERNAME:	
PASSWORD:	
EMAIL:	
CATEGORY:	
NOTE:	

	SITE
URL:	
USERNAME:	
PASSWORD:	
EMAIL:	
CATEGORY:	
NOTE:	

	SITE
URL:	
USERNAME:	
PASSWORD:	
EMAIL:	
CATEGORY:	
NOTE:	

SITE

URL:

USERNAME:

PASSWORD:

EMAIL:

CATEGORY:

NOTE:

SITE

URL:

USERNAME:

PASSWORD:

EMAIL:

CATEGORY:

NOTE:

SITE

URL:

USERNAME:

PASSWORD:

EMAIL:

CATEGORY:

NOTE:

SITE

URL:

USERNAME:

PASSWORD:

EMAIL:

CATEGORY:

NOTE:

SITE

URL:

USERNAME:

PASSWORD:

EMAIL:

CATEGORY:

NOTE:

SITE

URL:

USERNAME:

PASSWORD:

EMAIL:

CATEGORY:

NOTE:

SITE

URL:

USERNAME:

PASSWORD:

EMAIL:

CATEGORY:

NOTE:

SITE

URL:

USERNAME:

PASSWORD:

EMAIL:

CATEGORY:

NOTE:

SITE

URL:

USERNAME:

PASSWORD:

EMAIL:

CATEGORY:

NOTE:

SITE

URL:

USERNAME:

PASSWORD:

EMAIL:

CATEGORY:

NOTE:

SITE

URL:

USERNAME:

PASSWORD:

EMAIL:

CATEGORY:

NOTE:

SITE

URL:

USERNAME:

PASSWORD:

EMAIL:

CATEGORY:

NOTE:

SITE

URL:

USERNAME:

PASSWORD:

EMAIL:

CATEGORY:

NOTE:

SITE

URL:

USERNAME:

PASSWORD:

EMAIL:

CATEGORY:

NOTE:

SITE

URL:

USERNAME:

PASSWORD:

EMAIL:

CATEGORY:

NOTE:

SITE

URL:

USERNAME:

PASSWORD:

EMAIL:

CATEGORY:

NOTE:

SITE

URL:

USERNAME:

PASSWORD:

EMAIL:

CATEGORY:

NOTE:

SITE

URL:

USERNAME:

PASSWORD:

EMAIL:

CATEGORY:

NOTE:

SITE

URL:

USERNAME:

PASSWORD:

EMAIL:

CATEGORY:

NOTE:

SITE

URL:

USERNAME:

PASSWORD:

EMAIL:

CATEGORY:

NOTE:

SITE

URL:

USERNAME:

PASSWORD:

EMAIL:

CATEGORY:

NOTE:

SITE

URL:

USERNAME:

PASSWORD:

EMAIL:

CATEGORY:

NOTE:

SITE

URL:

USERNAME:

PASSWORD:

EMAIL:

CATEGORY:

NOTE:

SITE

URL:

USERNAME:

PASSWORD:

EMAIL:

CATEGORY:

NOTE:

SITE	
URL:	
USERNAME:	
PASSWORD:	
EMAIL:	
CATEGORY:	
NOTE:	

SITE	
URL:	
USERNAME:	
PASSWORD:	
EMAIL:	
CATEGORY:	
NOTE:	

SITE	
URL:	
USERNAME:	
PASSWORD:	
EMAIL:	
CATEGORY:	
NOTE:	

SITE	
URL:	
USERNAME:	
PASSWORD:	
EMAIL:	
CATEGORY:	
NOTE:	

SITE

URL:

USERNAME:

PASSWORD:

EMAIL:

CATEGORY:

NOTE:

SITE

URL:

USERNAME:

PASSWORD:

EMAIL:

CATEGORY:

NOTE:

SITE

URL:

USERNAME:

PASSWORD:

EMAIL:

CATEGORY:

NOTE:

SITE

URL:

USERNAME:

PASSWORD:

EMAIL:

CATEGORY:

NOTE:

SITE	
URL:	
USERNAME:	
PASSWORD:	
EMAIL:	
CATEGORY:	
NOTE:	

SITE	
URL:	
USERNAME:	
PASSWORD:	
EMAIL:	
CATEGORY:	
NOTE:	

SITE	
URL:	
USERNAME:	
PASSWORD:	
EMAIL:	
CATEGORY:	
NOTE:	

SITE	
URL:	
USERNAME:	
PASSWORD:	
EMAIL:	
CATEGORY:	
NOTE:	

SITE

URL:

USERNAME:

PASSWORD:

EMAIL:

CATEGORY:

NOTE:

SITE

URL:

USERNAME:

PASSWORD:

EMAIL:

CATEGORY:

NOTE:

SITE

URL:

USERNAME:

PASSWORD:

EMAIL:

CATEGORY:

NOTE:

SITE

URL:

USERNAME:

PASSWORD:

EMAIL:

CATEGORY:

NOTE:

SITE	
URL:	
USERNAME:	
PASSWORD:	
EMAIL:	
CATEGORY:	
NOTE:	

SITE	
URL:	
USERNAME:	
PASSWORD:	
EMAIL:	
CATEGORY:	
NOTE:	

SITE	
URL:	
USERNAME:	
PASSWORD:	
EMAIL:	
CATEGORY:	
NOTE:	

SITE	
URL:	
USERNAME:	
PASSWORD:	
EMAIL:	
CATEGORY:	
NOTE:	

SITE

URL:

USERNAME:

PASSWORD:

EMAIL:

CATEGORY:

NOTE:

SITE

URL:

USERNAME:

PASSWORD:

EMAIL:

CATEGORY:

NOTE:

SITE

URL:

USERNAME:

PASSWORD:

EMAIL:

CATEGORY:

NOTE:

SITE

URL:

USERNAME:

PASSWORD:

EMAIL:

CATEGORY:

NOTE:

SITE

URL:

USERNAME:

PASSWORD:

EMAIL:

CATEGORY:

NOTE:

SITE

URL:

USERNAME:

PASSWORD:

EMAIL:

CATEGORY:

NOTE:

SITE

URL:

USERNAME:

PASSWORD:

EMAIL:

CATEGORY:

NOTE:

SITE

URL:

USERNAME:

PASSWORD:

EMAIL:

CATEGORY:

NOTE:

SITE	
URL:	
USERNAME:	
PASSWORD:	
EMAIL:	
CATEGORY:	
NOTE:	

SITE	
URL:	
USERNAME:	
PASSWORD:	
EMAIL:	
CATEGORY:	
NOTE:	

SITE	
URL:	
USERNAME:	
PASSWORD:	
EMAIL:	
CATEGORY:	
NOTE:	

SITE	
URL:	
USERNAME:	
PASSWORD:	
EMAIL:	
CATEGORY:	
NOTE:	

NOTE:

NOTE:

ADDRESS:

USERNAME:

PASSWORD:

NOTE:

:

ADDRESS:

USERNAME:

PASSWORD:

NOTE::

HARDWARE LICENSE NUMBERS

1.
2.
3.
4.
5.
6.

HARDWARE LICENSE NUMBERS

1.
2.
3.
4.
5.
6.

SOFTWARE LICENSE NUMBERS

1.
2.
3.
4.
5.
6.

SOFTWARE LICENSE NUMBERS

1.
2.
3.
4.
5.
6.

SMARTPHONE:

1.
2.
3.
4.
5.
6.

SMARTWATCH:

1.
2.
3.
4.
5.
6.

SMART FITNESS:

1.
2.
3.
4.
5.
6.

SMART APPLIANCE:

1.
2.
3.
4.
5.
6.

SMART APPLIANCE:

1.
2.
3.
4.
5.
NOTE:

SMART APPLIANCE:

1.
2.
3.
4.
5.
NOTE:

SMART APPLIANCE:

1.
2.
3.
4.
5.
NOTE:

SMART APPLIANCE:

1.
2.
3.
4.
5.
NOTE:

NOTES
NOTES
NOTES
NOTES

NOTES
NOTES
NOTES
NOTES

NOTES
NOTES
NOTES
NOTES

NOTES

NOTES

NOTES

NOTES

Made in the USA
Monee, IL
07 July 2026